To:

_____

From:

_____

Date:

_____

Gods

Little
ANSWER
Book

WORD PUBLISHING
Dallas • London • Vancouver • Melbourne

Library of Congress Cataloging-in-Publication Data:
God's little answer book.
p.   cm.
ISBN 0-8499-5156-9
1. Christian life—Quotations, maxims, etc. 2. Bible—Quotations.
I. Word Publishing.
BV4513.G635   1995
242—dc20
95-19187
CIP

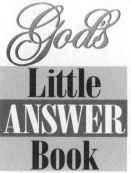

$\mathscr{F}$aith can come to those who
peer over the cliff and climb down slowly
as well as to those who take a single leap
from the mountain's edge.

Most assuredly, I say to you, he who hears
My word and believes in Him who sent Me has
everlasting life, and shall not come into judgment,
but has passed from death into life.

JOHN 5:24

$\mathcal{M}$any things may capture your
eye—let faith in God capture your heart.

*Therefore whoever confesses Me before men, him I will
also confess before My Father who is in heaven.*

MATTHEW 10:32

Only the rare grain of sand is destined to become a pearl. To God you are that special grain of sand—designed for eternity.

He who finds his life will lose it, and he who loses his life for My sake will find it.

MATTHEW 10:39

$\mathcal{C}$hrist goes before us and leaves
His footprints to guide us. Then He takes
our hand and walks with us.

*And those who are Christ's have crucified the
flesh with its passions and desires. If we live in the
Spirit, let us also walk in the Spirit.*

GALATIANS 5:24, 25

Even a seed of faith can grow in the
crack of a rock if it keeps its face to the sun.

But he who received seed on the good ground is
he who hears the word and understands it,
who indeed bears fruit and produces: some a
hundredfold, some sixty, some thirty.

MATTHEW 13:23

$\mathcal{I}$f you let Him, God will transform your personal prison into a penthouse of praise.

I will give you a new heart and put a new spirit within you; I will take the heart of stone out of your flesh and give you a heart of flesh.

EZEKIEL 36:26

$\mathcal{W}$e cannot build a ladder high enough
to reach God. He reaches down to touch us.

For by grace you have been saved through faith,
and that not of yourselves; it is the gift of God, . . .

EPHESIANS 2:8

$\mathcal{D}$on't trade heaven's eternal treasures
for the earth's limited pleasures—the one
cannot be lost, the other cannot be kept.

*I have been crucified with Christ; it is no longer
I who live, but Christ lives in me; and the life which
I now live in the flesh I live by faith in the Son of God,
who loved me and gave Himself for me.*

GALATIANS 2:20

$\mathcal{T}$he Christian church began against overwhelming odds, but nothing could defeat it.

Fight the good fight of faith, lay hold on eternal life, to which you were also called and have confessed the good confession in the presence of many witnesses.

1 TIMOTHY 6:12

*I*t's natural to be religious;
it's supernatural to know Jesus and
to make Him your Lord.

Jesus answered and said to him,
"Most assuredly, I say to you, unless one is born again,
he cannot see the kingdom of God."

JOHN 3:3

$\mathcal{W}$hen you study the Bible hit and miss,
you miss more than you hit.

*Let the word of Christ dwell in you richly in
all wisdom, teaching and admonishing one another
in psalms and hymns and spiritual songs, singing
with grace in your hearts to the Lord.*

COLOSSIANS 3:16

$\mathcal{S}$weet water is flowing water.
Plant your heart by the stream of God's love
and you will drink anew every day.

*And Jesus said to them, "I am the bread of life.
He who comes to Me shall never hunger, and he who
believes in Me shall never thirst."*

JOHN 6:35

$\mathscr{T}$he Bible is like a practical repair manual: there are no hopeless cases and always room for improvement.

And He said to me, "My grace is sufficient for you, for My strength is made perfect in weakness." Therefore most gladly I will rather boast in my infirmities, that the power of Christ may rest upon me.

2 CORINTHIANS 12:9

$\mathscr{H}$ell is locked from the outside,
heaven from the inside. Could it be
because no one chooses to leave heaven,
and no one wants to remain in hell?

He laid His right hand on me, saying to me,
"Do not be afraid; I am the First and the Last. I am He
who lives, and was dead, and behold, I am alive forevermore.
Amen. And I have the keys of Hades and of Death."

REVELATION 1:17–18

*H*ide and Seek is no game to
play with God. You either hide from Him
like Adam, or you seek after Him like David.

You will seek the LORD your God,
and you will find Him if you seek Him with all
your heart and with all your soul.

DEUTERONOMY 4:29

$\mathscr{A}$ lie is worth nothing;
the truth has value beyond description.

*And you shall know the truth, and the truth
shall make you free. Therefore if the Son makes
you free, you shall be free indeed.*

JOHN 8:32, 36

$\mathcal{G}$od's arm is long enough to reach into the mouth of a lion or the belly of a whale. If you but ask, God will roll up His sleeves and meet your need.

But the Lord stood with me and strengthened me, so that the message might be preached fully through me, and that all the Gentiles might hear. Also I was delivered out of the mouth of the lion.

2 TIMOTHY 4:17

$\mathcal{F}$aith is not believing God can do it—
it is knowing that He will.

My help comes from the Lord, who made
heaven and earth. He will not allow your foot to be
moved; He who keeps you will not slumber.

PSALM 121:2, 3

*L*ong before the well runs dry,
the water may turn bitter. Jesus is
eternally refreshing, let Him quench
your spiritual thirst.

*Now Jacob's well was there. Jesus therefore,
being wearied from His journey, sat thus by the well.
It was about the sixth hour.*

JOHN 4:6

$\mathcal{T}$here is no trouble troubling
you that God has not already solved.

The LORD shall preserve you from all evil;
He shall preserve your soul. The LORD shall
preserve your going out and your coming in from
this time forth, and even forevermore.

PSALM 121:7, 8

$\mathcal{I}$t takes two to quarrel,
but only one to apologize.

*Fulfill my joy by being like-minded, having
the same love, being of one accord, of one mind.*

PHILIPPIANS 2:2

To have a friend, be a friend.
To have an enemy, be an enemy.

*But if we walk in the light as He is in the light,
we have fellowship with one another,
and the blood of Jesus Christ His Son
cleanses us from all sin.*

1 JOHN 1:7

Forgetfulness is one of the devil's favorite tools. Remember what God has done for you in the past and expect new blessings from Him today.

Your word I have hidden in my heart,
that I might not sin against You.
I will delight myself in Your statutes;
I will not forget Your word.

PSALM 119:11, 16

The best gift you can
give your grandchildren is to take
their parents to church.

The words of the LORD are pure words,
like silver tried in a furnace of earth, purified
seven times. You shall keep them, O LORD, You shall
preserve them from this generation forever.

PSALM 12:6, 7

The one who dares to trust God
is the only one who knows how to live.

But He answered and said, "It is written,
'Man shall not live by bread alone, but by every
word that proceeds from the mouth of God.'"

MATTHEW 4:4

God keeps no secrets from sinners.
But sinners think they can keep secrets
from God.

Would not God search this out?
For He knows the secrets of the heart.

PSALM 44:21

Worry changes nothing;
prayer changes everything.

If you abide in Me, and My words abide in you,
you will ask what you desire, and it shall be done for you.

JOHN 15:7

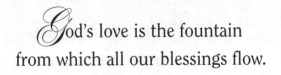

God's love is the fountain
from which all our blessings flow.

I love those who love me,
and those who seek me diligently will find me.

PROVERBS 8:17

$\mathcal{S}$elfless praying leads to selfless living.
Your heart will grow in the direction
of your prayers.

I will meditate on Your precepts,
and contemplate Your ways. I will delight myself in
Your statutes; I will not forget Your word.

PSALM 119:15, 16

Courage is the price God asks from us
on the way to granting us peace.

Draw near to God and He will draw
near to you. Cleanse your hands, you sinners;
and purify your hearts, you double-minded.

JAMES 4:8

$\mathcal{I}$t costs you nothing to
become a Christian. It may cost you
everything to be a Christian.

Have I not commanded you?
Be strong and of good courage; do not be afraid,
nor be dismayed, for the LORD your God is with
you wherever you go.

JOSHUA 1:9

$\mathcal{G}$od has wagered He can
make something great of you;
the devil has gambled that you will fail.
Your actions will prove one of them right.

What then shall we say to these things?
If God is for us, who can be against us?

ROMANS 8:31

*W*hy can some people
believe in the promises of the lottery
and not in the promises of God?

*Jesus said to him, "If you can believe,
all things are possible to him who believes."*

MARK 9:23

$\mathcal{Y}$ou will never be the person
God wants you to be until you do what
God wants you to do.

*For all things are for your sakes,
that grace, having spread through the many,
may cause thanksgiving to abound to the glory of God.
Therefore we do not lose heart. Even though our
outward man is perishing, yet the inward man is
being renewed day by day.*

2 CORINTHIANS 4:15, 16

$\mathcal{T}$he wages of sin may be tax-free,
but they're not carefree. The sins of the past
place a heavy burden on an unforgiven heart.

For to be carnally minded is death,
but to be spiritually minded is life and peace.

ROMANS 8:6

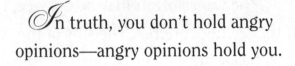

*I*n truth, you don't hold angry
opinions—angry opinions hold you.

*Whoever has no rule over his own spirit
is like a city broken down, without walls.*

PROVERBS 25:28

$\mathcal{P}$eople don't plan to spend eternity
without God, but without a change in
direction, that is exactly what they will do.

There is a way that seems right to a man,
but its end is the way of death.

PROVERBS 14:12

A prayer is a wish turned upward.
Hold good things to your heart
and your spirit will flourish.

Finally, brethren, whatever things are true,
whatever things are noble, whatever things are just,
whatever things pure, whatever things are lovely,
whatever things are of good report, if there is any
virtue and if there is anything praiseworthy—
mediate on these things.

PHILIPPIANS 4:8

$\mathcal{D}$o what you can;
your heavenly Father will do
what you can't.

*I can do all things through
Christ who strengthens me.*

PHILIPPIANS 4:13

$\mathcal{A}$ curse is a prayer to the devil.
Think twice before you vent your anger
on someone—and then think again.

Be angry, and do not sin:
do not let the sun go down on your wrath,
nor give place to the devil.

EPHESIANS 4:26, 27

The difference between good and evil is often the difference between humility and arrogance. When you begin to think you're above God, it's a sure sign you're not.

And the Lord will deliver me from every evil work and preserve me for His heavenly kingdom. To Him be glory forever and ever. Amen!

2 TIMOTHY 4:18

$\mathcal{M}$ost of what you worry about
never happens . . . and what does happen
is usually so unexpected you wouldn't
have thought to worry about it anyway.

Therefore do not worry about tomorrow,
for tomorrow will worry about its own things.
Sufficient for the day is its own trouble.

MATTHEW 6:34

$\mathscr{A}$ sheep never teases a wolf.
It knows you can't play with the enemy
and not suffer the consequences.

*Behold, I send you out as sheep
in the midst of wolves. Therefore be wise
as serpents and harmless as doves.*

MATTHEW 10:16

The word *gospel* begins
with *go*. A faith worth believing is
a faith worth sharing.

And he said to them, "Go ye into all the world,
and preach the gospel to every creature."

MARK 16:15

$\mathcal{T}$he Bible teaches us the
best way to live . . . and provides
the only way to die.

For God has not given us a spirit of fear,
but of power and of love and of a sound mind.

2 Timothy 1:7

$\mathcal{H}$ell has no exits,
and heaven needs none.

No one can serve two masters;
for either he will hate the one and love the other,
or else he will be loyal to the one and despise the other.
You cannot serve God and mammon.

MATTHEW 6:24

If you are hitting your target too easily, perhaps you are not challenging yourself enough. Those with great inner purpose succeed in life.

*And do not be conformed to this world,
but be transformed by the renewing of your mind,
that you may prove what is that good and
acceptable and perfect will of God.*

ROMANS 12:2

$\mathscr{J}$ust as an old horse knows the
way home, so a "seasoned" sinner finds
it easier to transgress than to do good.
On the contrary, a saint of many years has
purposely established habits of goodness and
finds virtue the more sensible course.

*Then the Lord knows how to deliver the godly
out of temptations and to reserve the unjust under
punishment for the day of judgment.*

2 PETER 2:9

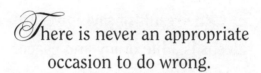

There is never an appropriate occasion to do wrong.

Set your mind on things above,
not on things on the earth.

COLOSSIANS 3:2

The result of saying yes to
Jesus is a life of joy and peace.
Make Him your first choice.

Who is he who overcomes the world,
but he who believes that Jesus is the Son of God?

1 JOHN 5:5

$\mathcal{O}$nly fools buy what they do not need, with money they do not have, to impress people who do not even care.

And He said to them, "Take heed and beware of covetousness, for one's life does not consist in the abundance of the things he possesses."

LUKE 12:15

A parked car gets no speeding tickets, nor does it cover any distance. Give up your fear of making mistakes and let God's power give you life abundant.

These things I have spoken to you, that in Me you may have peace. In the world you will have tribulation; but be of good cheer, I have overcome the world.

JOHN 16:33

$\mathcal{T}$emptations seldom come through
the front door of life. They slip through
open windows and slide down the chimney.

*No temptation has overtaken you except
such as is common to man; but God is faithful,
who will not allow you to be tempted beyond what
you are able, but with the temptation will also make
the way of escape, that you may be able to bear it.*

1 CORINTHIANS 10:13

$\mathcal{B}$e content with what you have,
but never with who you are.

*I say then: Walk in the Spirit, and you
shall not fulfill the lust of the flesh. For the flesh
lusts against the Spirit, and the Spirit against the flesh;
and these are contrary to one another, so that you
do not do the things that you wish.*

GALATIANS 5:16, 17

$\mathcal{T}$he only way to escape from
the devil is to flee into the arms of God.

Therefore submit to God.
Resist the devil and he will flee from you.

JAMES 4:7

$\mathcal{T}$hose who are weak see themselves as slaves of fate; the strong live above their circumstances.

My brethren, count it all joy when you fall into various trials, knowing that the testing of your faith produces patience. But let patience have its perfect work, that you may be perfect and complete, lacking nothing.

JAMES 1:2–4

A flawed emerald is still of greater value than a perfectly cut brick.

Pride goes before destruction, and a haughty spirit before a fall. Better to be of a humble spirit with the lowly, than to divide the spoil with the proud.

PROVERBS 16:18, 19

$\mathcal{M}$uch of what you do in
life may not take on great significance.
But still you must do it. It is the path to
true greatness and personal growth.

Yet it shall not be so among you;
but whoever desires to become great among you,
let him be your servant. And whoever desires to be
first among you, let him be your slave.

MATTHEW 20:26, 27

This is your day to slow down,
reflect on your life, and let God love
you as never before.

*Take My yoke upon you and learn
from Me, for I am gentle and lowly in heart,
and you will find rest for your souls. For My yoke
is easy and My burden is light.*

MATTHEW 11:29, 30

$\mathcal{A}$ccept all honors and rewards with your head humbly bowed. God is the source of all good things that come our way.

*By humility and the fear of the L*ORD
are riches and honor and life.

PROVERBS 22:4

A sharp tongue is seldom
the indication of a sharp mind.

Death and life are in the power of the tongue,
and those who love it will eat its fruit.

PROVERBS 18:21

$\mathcal{B}$e sure the welcome mat outside your door is not false advertising. Hospitality comes from the inside or it doesn't come at all.

Let all bitterness, wrath, anger, clamor,
and evil speaking be put away from you, with all malice.

EPHESIANS 4:31

The difference between fishing
for fish and fishing for people is that a
fisherman catches living fish and they die;
an evangelist catches those who are dead
in spirit and shows them how to live.

The LORD has made known His salvation;
His righteousness He has revealed in the
sight of the nations.

PSALM 98:2

*Y*our tongue is attached to
your heart. Not to speak ill of another
requires only silence.

*As long as my breath is in me, and the breath
of God in my nostrils, my lips will not speak
wickedness, nor my tongue utter deceit.*

JOB 27:3, 4

*H*ow you choose to let God love you
today determines how you will
love others tomorrow.

*Seek the LORD and His strength; seek His face
evermore! Remember His marvelous works which He
has done, His wonders, and the judgments of His mouth.*

1 CHRONICLES 16:11, 12

$\mathcal{T}$ake a microscope to God and search vainly for any imperfection; take a magnifying glass to the devil and search vainly for any perfection.

Oh, magnify the LORD with me, and let us exalt His name together. I sought the LORD, and He heard me, and delivered me from all my fears.

PSALM 34:3, 4

*Y*our faith in Christ is bread for
daily use, not dessert for special occasions.

For You are my hope, O Lord GOD; You are my
trust from my youth. Let my mouth be filled with
Your praise and with Your glory all the day.

PSALM 71:5, 8

*Y*ou sing off key when you sing your own praises. Give praise to God and you'll join a harmonious chorus.

It is good to give thanks to the LORD, and to sing praise to Your name, O Most High; to declare Your lovingkindness in the morning, . . .

PSALM 92:1, 2

To have God's power, you must
be plugged into God's love.

I will sing to the LORD as long as I live;
I will sing praise to my God while I have my being.

PSALM 104:33

*Y*ou have an everlasting destiny.
Today truly is the first day of
the rest of your eternal life.

You will keep him in perfect peace, whose
mind is stayed on You, because he trusts in You.

ISAIAH 26:3

The cross was an instrument of death until Christ made it an instrument of life.

The He said to them all, "If anyone desires to come after Me, let him deny himself, and take up his cross daily, and follow Me. For whoever desires to save his life will lose it, but whoever loses his life for My sake will save it."

LUKE 9:23, 24

$\mathcal{I}$f you would be free, seek
purpose rather than freedom. Freedom
without direction breeds confusion; freedom
with purpose leads to personal greatness.

*For you, brethren, have been called to liberty;
only do not use liberty as an opportunity for the
flesh, but through love serve one another.*

GALATIANS 5:13

$\mathcal{G}$od never asks how many
people are serving you. He asks how
many people you are serving.

*For though I am free from all men, I have made
myself a servant to all, that I might win the more.*

1 Corinthians 9:19

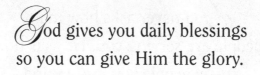

*G*od gives you daily blessings
so you can give Him the glory.

*Because Your lovingkindness is better
than life, my lips shall praise You.*

PSALM 63:3

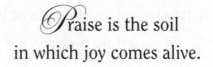

$\mathscr{P}$raise is the soil
in which joy comes alive.

Praise the LORD! Praise God in His sanctuary;
praise Him in His mighty firmament!

PSALM 150:1

$\mathcal{I}$t is better to err on the side of kindness. A tongue of praise has no time for gossip.

Whoever offers praise glorifies Me; and to him who orders his conduct aright I will show the salvation of God.

PSALM 50:23

$\mathcal{I}$f you envy your neighbors' shoes, be prepared to share their corns and calluses.

Let your conduct be without covetousness; be content with such things as you have. For He Himself has said, "I will never leave you nor forsake you."

HEBREWS 13:5

$\mathscr{S}$ing and be thankful. God delights in the joyous praise of His children.

Praise the LORD! Praise the LORD, O my soul!
While I live I will praise the LORD; I will sing
praises to my God while I have my being.

PSALM 146:1, 2

The size of your world
is the size of your heart.

*His lord said to him, "Well done, good and
faithful servant; you were faithful over a few
things, I will make you ruler over many things.
Enter into the joy of your lord."*

MATTHEW 25:21

$\mathcal{L}$ove is a chain reaction: The one you love is free to love another. This is God's divine care network.

These things I have spoken to you, that My joy may remain in you, and that your joy may be full. This is My commandment, that you love one another as I have loved you.

JOHN 15:11, 12

*R*evival is the Spirit of God
poured into human vessels.

*Restore to me the joy of Your salvation, and
uphold me by Your generous Spirit. Then I will
teach transgressors Your ways, and sinners
shall be converted to You.*

PSALM 51:12, 13

To stub your toe doesn't mean you are walking in the wrong direction. God doesn't promise a path without trouble. He promises a journey worth the trouble.

Yet if anyone suffers as a Christian, let him not be ashamed, but let him glorify God in this matter.

1 PETER 4:16

$\mathcal{T}$he rich must learn they have little
that God wants. The poor must understand
they already possess what He desires.

*For He satisfies the longing soul, and fills
the hungry soul with goodness.*

PSALM 107:9

God is in the recycling business.
Instead of throwing us out, He cleans
us up until we shine like new! Thank
God, we always have hope in Him.

*Create in me a clean heart, O God, and renew a
steadfast spirit within me. Do not cast me away from
Your presence, and do not take Your Holy Spirit from
me. Restore to me the joy of Your salvation, and
uphold me by Your generous Spirit.*

PSALM 51:10–12

The sweetest song can come
from a broken heart.

In God I have put my trust; I will not be afraid.
Have You not kept my feet from falling, that I may
walk before God in the light of the living?

PSALM 56:11, 13

To master temptation, let God master you; your best escape to freedom is the pursuit of that which is good.

Blessed is the man who endures temptation; for when he has been proved, he will receive the crown of life which the Lord has promised to those who love Him.

JAMES 1:12

To be a servant of others, God will first make you master of yourself.

By this we know love, because He laid down His life for us. And we also ought to lay down our lives for the brethren.

1 JOHN 3:16

$\mathscr{G}$ood news! When you look into a mirror
you see someone created in the image
of God. It's a great way to start the day!

*But you are a chosen generation, a royal priesthood,
a holy nation, His own special people, that you may
proclaim the praises of Him who called you out
of darkness into His marvelous light.*

1 PETER 2:9

$\mathcal{M}$ake suffering a magnet
that draws you closer to God.

*My brethren, take the prophets, who spoke
in the name of the Lord, as an example
of suffering and patience.*

JAMES 5:10

$\mathcal{B}$ecause God wanted more children,
He searched the whole earth and found you.
You are precious in His sight.

Trust in the LORD, and do good;
dwell in the land, and feed on His faithfulness.
Delight yourself also in the LORD, and He shall
give you the desires of your heart.

PSALM 37:3, 4

When you belong to Christ, all you possess belongs to Him. The true measure of your riches is what will be yours in eternity.

For the love of money is a root of all kinds of evil. . . . But you, O man of God, flee these things and pursue righteousness, godliness, faith, love, patience, gentleness.

1 Timothy 6:10, 11

The rich look at God and wonder what He will ask of them. The poor approach God and ask what they can offer Him.

The young lions lack and suffer hunger; but those who seek the LORD shall not lack any good thing.

PSALM 34:10

$\mathcal{P}$ray as you ought, and you will live as you pray. God will create a new spirit in you and will revive your enthusiasm for living!

Fear not, for I am with you; be not dismayed, for I am your God, I will strengthen you, yes, I will help you, I will uphold you with My righteous right hand.

ISAIAH 41:10

$\mathcal{R}$epentance is more than saying
"I'm sorry." It is also saying "I'm through."

*Do you not know that friendship with the world is
enmity with God? Whoever therefore wants
to be a friend of the world makes
himself an enemy of God.*

JAMES 4:4

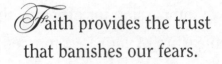

$\mathcal{F}$aith provides the trust
that banishes our fears.

And let us not grow weary while doing good, for
in due season we shall reap if we do not lose heart.

GALATIANS 6:9

$\mathcal{C}$ompassion for others is the
measure of your love for God.

*And we have known and believed the love
that God has for us. God is love, and he who abides
in love abides in God, and God in him.*

1 JOHN 4:16

$\mathscr{G}$od rewards you for a job well done by giving you an even bigger job.

Through the LORD's mercies we are not consumed, because His compassions fail not. They are new every morning; great is Your faithfulness.

LAMENTATIONS 3:22

$\mathcal{M}$ake your hopes big hopes.
God has designed you for greatness.

*Now may the God of hope fill you with all joy
and peace in believing, that you may abound
in hope by the power of the Holy Spirit.*

ROMANS 15:13

$\mathcal{M}$ake your dreams and desires worthy
of God's power to make them come true.

*Wait on the LORD; be of good courage, and He
shall strengthen your heart; wait, I say, on the LORD!*

PSALM 27:14

$\mathscr{G}$od's answers are wiser than our prayers. In all things let us pray for His will to be done.

He knelt down and prayed saying, "Father, if it is Your will, take this cup away from Me; nevertheless not My will, but Yours, be done."

LUKE 22:41, 42

*Y*ou will know the peace of God when you know the God of peace.

For God is not the author of confusion but of peace, as in all the churches of the saints.

1 CORINTHIANS 14:33

$\mathcal{L}$earn from those who are older.
Only foolish people find it necessary
to make all their own mistakes.

Furthermore, we have had human fathers who corrected us, and we paid them respect. Shall we not much more readily be in subjection to the Father of spirits and live?

HEBREWS 12:9

"*In* God We Trust" is written on your money. Carve it on your heart as well.

He who dwells in the secret place of the Most High shall abide under the shadow of the Almighty. I will say of the LORD, He is my refuge and my fortress; My God, in Him I will trust.

PSALM 91:1, 2

$\mathscr{W}$hat you weave on earth,
you will wear in eternity.

*Those who are wise shall shine like the brightness
of the firmament, and those who turn many to
righteousness like the stars forever and ever.*

DANIEL 12:3

$\mathcal{O}$nly the foolish and the dead
refuse to change their opinions. Ask God
to keep you open to fresh, new ideas.

He who heeds the word wisely will find good,
and whoever trusts in the LORD, happy is he.

PROVERBS 16:20

*I*f you lose your faith, you lose everything. When you find faith, you find everything that matters.

For none of us lives to himself, and no one dies to himself. For if we live, we live to the Lord; and if we die, we die to the Lord. Therefore, whether we live or die, we are the Lord's.

ROMANS 14:7, 8

$\mathcal{T}$here is no map to heaven.
You reach it with the help of a personal
guide—the Holy Spirit.

For this is God, our God forever and ever;
He will be our guide even to death.

PSALM 48:14

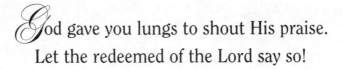

God gave you lungs to shout His praise.
Let the redeemed of the Lord say so!

But let all those rejoice who put their trust in You;
let them ever shout for joy, because You defend
them; Let those also who love Your name
be joyful in You.

PSALM 5:11

$\mathcal{G}$od welcomes all personal requests. He is eager to know the desires of your heart. You are His beloved, and He is yours.

Be anxious for nothing, but in everything by prayer and supplication, with thanksgiving, let your requests be made known to God; and the peace of God, which surpasses all understanding, will guard your hearts and minds through Christ Jesus.

PHILIPPIANS 4:6, 7

God knows that deep roots and healthy branches are developed in all manner of wind and weather. Trust Him in the sunshine and believe Him in the storms.

The LORD will guide you continually, and satisfy your soul in drought, and strengthen your bones; you shall be like a watered garden, and like a spring of water, whose waters do not fail.

ISAIAH 58:11

The richest people in the world are those who are content with what they have—no matter how little it may be.

Now godliness with contentment is great gain. For we brought nothing into this world, and it is certain we can carry nothing out. And having food and clothing, with these we shall be content.

1 TIMOTHY 6:6–8

$\mathcal{L}$et the author of your faith be
the author of your day. Your own rules
and regulations must not replace
God's requirements.

*Abide in Me, and I in you. As the branch cannot
bear fruit of itself, unless it abides in the vine,
neither can you, unless you abide in Me.*

JOHN 15:4

$\mathscr{E}$very day with God is like Christmas. Look under His tree of love and mercy for the gifts He has given you today.

As each one has received a gift, minister it to one another, as good stewards of the manifold grace of God.

1 PETER 4:10

$\mathcal{G}$od searched throughout the universe until He found you. Before you were born, He wanted you to be part of His intimate family.

You did not choose Me, but I chose you and appointed you that you should go and bear fruit, and that your fruit should remain, that whatever you ask the Father in My name He may give you. These things I command you, that you love one another.

JOHN 15:16, 17

A single word from God set the universe in motion. That same God of creation is your heavenly Father. Be the person He designed you to be.

So shall My word be that goes forth from My mouth; it shall not return to Me void, but it shall accomplish what I please, and it shall prosper in the thing for which I sent it.

Isaiah 55:11

$\mathcal{F}$aith is the simple awareness that God *is*,
and that He will *do* what He promises.

*Now this is the confidence that we have in Him, that
if we ask anything according to His will, He hears us.
And if we know that He hears us, whatever we ask,
we know that we have the petitions that
we have asked of Him.*

1 JOHN 5:14, 15

$\mathcal{G}$reat accomplishments are
simply small things carried out
with a desire to please God.

No one, when he has lit a lamp, puts it in a secret
place or under a basket, but on a lampstand, that
those who come in may see the light.

LUKE 11:33

$\mathcal{K}$eep God's commands in
your head and His love in your heart.

*Be diligent to present yourself approved
to God, a worker who does not need to be ashamed,
rightly dividing the word of truth.*

2 TIMOTHY 2:15

$\mathscr{H}$ot words cool friendships.
Control your tongue and you
control your life.

And a servant of the Lord must not
quarrel but be gentle to all, able to teach, patient,
in humility correcting those who are in opposition,
if God perhaps will grant them repentance,
so that they may know the truth.

2 TIMOTHY 2:24, 25

The world honors success;
God honors faithfulness.

For in it the righteousness of God is
revealed from faith to faith; as it is written,
The just shall live by faith.

ROMANS 1:17

To speak kindly
is a tonic to the tongue.

*Let the words of my mouth and the meditation
of my heart be acceptable in Your sight, O LORD,
my strength and my Redeemer.*

PSALM 19:14

$\mathscr{F}$aith gives you peace for the past, grace for the present, and hope for the future.

Therefore, having been justified by faith, we have peace with God through our Lord Jesus Christ, through whom also we have access by faith into this grace in which we stand, and rejoice in hope of the glory of God.

ROMANS 5:1, 2

$\mathcal{G}$od will often hide His purposes
so you will live on His promises.

*The Lord is not slack concerning His promise,
as some count slackness, but is longsuffering toward
us, not willing that any should perish but that all
should come to repentance.*

2 PETER 3:9

$\mathcal{C}$ourage is more than the strength
to go on. It's going on—in the power of
God—even when no human strength remains.

*Though I walk in the midst of trouble, You will revive
me; You will stretch out Your hand against the wrath
of my enemies, and Your right hand will save me.*

PSALM 138:7

The wise wait on God; the foolish
believe He should wait on them.

*Therefore the LORD will wait, that He may be
gracious to you; and therefore He will be exalted,
that He may have mercy on you. For the LORD is a
God of justice; blessed are all those who wait for Him.*

ISAIAH 30:18

To trust in God means you move ahead
with your heart when your head says
it can't be done.

*So you, by the help of your God, return; observe
mercy and justice, and wait on your God continually.*

HOSEA 12:6

$\mathscr{I}$t is a fact that one day you will die. The question is, how then will you live?

That all the peoples of the earth may know that the LORD is God; there is no other. Let your heart therefore be loyal to the LORD our God, to walk in His statutes and keep His commandments, as at this day.

1 KINGS 8:60, 61

$\mathcal{L}$ife's victories are won in inches, not miles. It is daily obedience to God that makes the difference.

Now therefore, if you will indeed obey My voice and keep My covenant, then you shall be a special treasure to Me above all people; for all the earth is Mine.

EXODUS 19:5

$\mathscr{S}$incere prayers have great power—wishes alone have none. Pray and God will answer.

So I say to you, ask, and it will be given to you; seek, and you will find; knock, and it will be opened to you. For everyone who asks receives, and he who seeks finds, and to him who knocks it will be opened.

LUKE 11:9, 10

$\mathcal{O}$nly by going God's
way will we know God's will.

*If you are willing and obedient, you shall
eat the good of the land; but if you refuse and rebel,
you shall be devoured by the sword; for the
mouth of the LORD has spoken.*

ISAIAH 1:19, 20

$\mathscr{N}$ever forget in the darkness what
God has taught you in the light.

*Happy are your men and happy are these
your servants, who stand continually
before you and hear your wisdom!*

2 CHRONICLES 9:7

$\mathcal{G}$ive God all He asks of you and be ready
to enjoy His promises for a lifetime.

*He who is faithful in what is least is faithful also
in much; and he who is unjust in what is least is
unjust also in much.*

LUKE 16:10

You will only *hear* God's voice
when you *listen* for God's voice.

*Behold, I stand at the door and knock. If anyone
hears My voice and opens the door, I will come in
to him and dine with him, and he with Me.*

REVELATION 3:20

*F*orgiveness means God buries
your sins in an unmarked grave.

*Let the wicked forsake his way, and the unrighteous
man his thoughts; let him return to the LORD, and
He will have mercy on him; and to our God, for He
will abundantly pardon.*

ISAIAH 55:7

$\mathscr{S}$in keeps you stumbling in the dark;
God's forgiveness lets you walk in the light.

*Have mercy upon me, O God, according to Your loving
kindness; according to the multitude of Your tender
mercies, blot out my transgressions. Wash me thoroughly
from my iniquity, and cleanse me from my sin.*

PSALM 51:1, 2

*G*reat trials precede great triumphs.
Affliction prepares us for extraordinary service.

Give ear, O LORD, to my prayer; and attend to
the voice of my supplications. In the day of my
trouble I will call upon You, for You will answer me.

PSALM 86:6, 7

*Other volumes to enoy from the
Moments for Your Life series:*

The Mirror Our Children See
Together Is Forever
Happiness Is . . .
God's Best for Your Success
God's Little Promise Book